AF504433

The Naughty Rotties

Mary Griffith Chalupsky

Published and Copyright 2022 by Corridor Publishing

marygriffithchalupskybooks.bigcartel.com

mary.chalupsky@yahoo.com

The publisher has no control or responsibility for third party websites or their content.

Special discounts are available on quantity purchases by corporations, schools, libraries, charities and others. For information on special discounts email the author at

mary.chalupsky@yahoo.com

Illustrator Mohsen Abdelhafiz

Author: Mary Griffith Chalupsky

Illustrator: Mohsen Abdelhafiz

The Naughty Rotties

Dedication

The door to the human heart can be opened only from the inside.

To Lori and Clay Tritle, who accepted Hansel and Gretel into their family with unconditional love.

Thank you,

Mary

Mama Rottie bathed the puppies each morning by licking them with her enormous tongue. Her nudges woke them and they knew it was time for breakfast.

The lady at the pet store dished up their meals, and both ate rapidly. They watched as their brothers and sisters were adopted. Now, it was time for the puppies, to begin a long journey to their new home.

Outside, the man drove up in his blue truck and went inside the pet store. All the dogs in the kennels barked in unison, as if to say, "pick me! pick me!"

He stopped at the desk and signed papers. Then the man and the lady walked toward the kennel and opened the gate. Both puppies squeezed through the hole... greeting the man with puppy kisses.

9

"Just look at you two. Cathy will love you both. would you like to come home with me?" he asked. The puppies were excited. The lady placed them in a box, and the man carried them to his truck. He placed the box in the cab and climbed in to drive them to their new home.

Arriving a short time later, both puppies were happy. The man wanted to surprise his wife, Cathy, so he left the puppies in the box and placed his shirt over them telling her it was his dirty laundry.

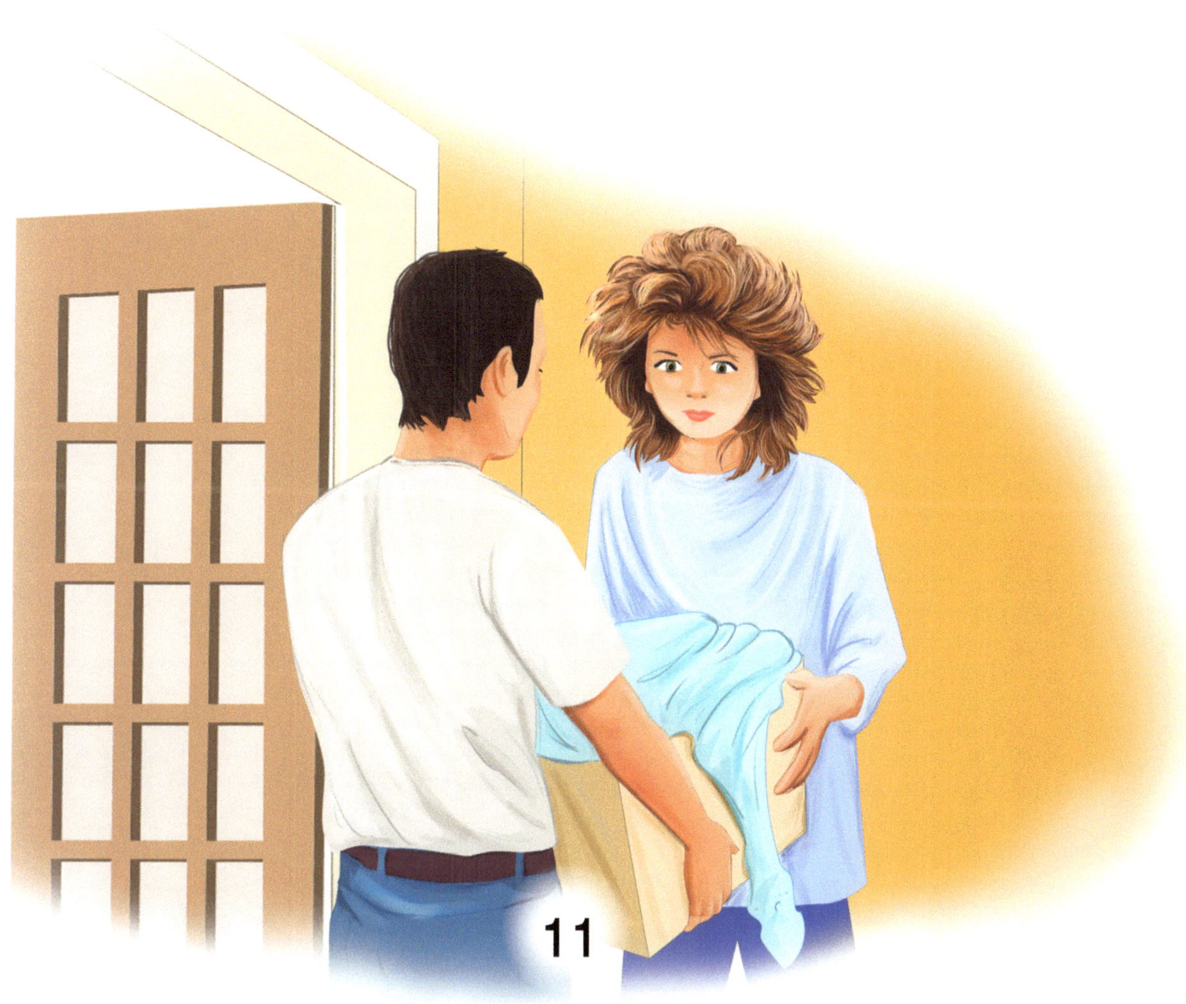

Cathy took the box to the laundry room and sat it on the floor. Removing the shirt to throw into the washing machine, she jumped when two puppy heads popped up. "Oh my! How cute you both are!" she exclaimed. Removing the puppies from the box, Cathy snuggled them close to her.

12

"I bet you're both a handful," she said. "I'm going to call you Hansel and Gretel. Those names will suit you fine. When I go to the pet store, I'll get you each a new bed. All pets should have their own space."

13

The puppies were happy with Mama Cathy and their new home.
They loved their sister Nicky, an Irish Setter.
Nicky already claimed the sofa as her special place.

14

The puppies followed Nicky all over the house. Nicky spent more time on the sofa than she did on the floor just to escape the puppies and their shenanigans.

15

Mama Cathy worked in her beauty parlor every day. She would come home midday to give the dogs attention. On occasion, she would arrive and discover the puppies had been naughty. They both chewed on everything, even though they owned many chew

toys. They chewed up the doggy gate in their bedroom. They learned how to turn on the shower in the guest bath. They would get scolded, then everything would be fine until it happened again. Mama Cathy knew she had to do something fast.

17

One day, as a diversion for the dogs, mama left the TV running while she was at work. When she came home, all three dogs were watching. She noticed they even watched when she was home. They became obsessed with, 'A Kingdom for Animals'. Mama Cathy was happy the dogs didn't know they were watching re-runs.

When Mama would come from work she always yelled, "where are my babies?" All three dogs would race to greet her at the door, wagging their tails.

19

One day Hansel and Gretel weren't feeling well. They were coughing and they refused to eat. Mama Cathy took them to the pet doctor or veterinarian. The doctor said they had Kennel Cough.

20

When they lived at the pet store and received their vaccinations, it was believed they received one for Kennel Cough. They were hospitalized for a long time. The puppies were happy to return home to Mama Cathy and sister Nicky when they were well.

One day, Mama Cathy explained to her dog babies that she must go away. Even though it made her sad, she couldn't take her beloved pets with her, but she explained to them they would be together again someday. She hugged Hansel, Gretel, and Nicky and told them when they were ready to cross the rainbow bridge, she would be waiting for them.

The dogs were sad, but they understood. A friend named Charlie volunteered to drive Hansel and Gretel to their new home in Iowa in his large van. As they were driving through the desert, Charlie stopped to let the dogs out to exercise.

Hansel slipped out of his collar and started roaming. Gretel followed, and both dogs started running, not knowing where they were going. Charlie chased after them, and the faster he ran the faster the dogs ran, Then Charlie remembered how to catch a runaway dog. He stopped running and laid perfectly still on the ground.

24

Hansel and Gretel stopped running and looked at him. They wondered why Charlie was lying on the ground. The dogs approached Charlie to take a closer look and he reached out and grabbed them. They returned to the van and continued their trip.

Arriving in Iowa they were greeted by Mama Lori and Daddy Clay who treated them warmly. Every day they received a topping on their food bowls of liverwurst, bologna, and a sprinkle of cheese.

Hansel and Gretel sniffed their new surroundings and decided it was a pretty nice place to be. There were acres of farmland and grassy slopes to investigate.

There were rabbits and squirrels that needed to play and many cornfields to be explored. They loved to wander off to the neighbors to play with their dogs. They loved it all. And a little girl called Audrey would occasionally come to play with them. Audrey called Hansel 'Handsome,' because she thought that was his name.

The years passed and Hansel and Gretel both became tired and slept most of the time. They were ready to cross the rainbow bridge together. Both remembered what Mama Cathy told them. As they crossed that colorful bridge, there was Mama Cathy with all of her precious pets. She was holding a large bone for each.

They ran toward her and she reached down and hugged them as she did the first time they met. Today, they are happy as they both sit with Mama Cathy beneath the ring bologna tree with a little liverwurst and cheese for flavor.

Catherine Mary Chalupsky Abbey

1955-2018

Missed by her family

BIOGRAPHY
Mary Griffith Chalupsky

Mary Griffith Chalupsky grew up in a little town in southern Illinois. She and her husband raised six children on a farm in central Iowa.

She won several awards during her lifetime through the World Poetry Association beginning in 1987 when she won the Golden Poet Award, the Silver Poet Award followed in 1990, and the Editor choice Award in 2005, 2006, and 2007.

Mary was a volunteer in her church, school and community for most of her life. She worked in the medical profession and owned and operated her own business, Medical Claims Billing. She is a member of the DAR and the Mayflower Society.

Presently she lives in Cedar Rapids, Iowa with her little dog Buttons, and she loves sitting on her back porch, working in her flower gardens and having coffee with her friends.

Mohsen Abdel Hafeez Abdel Aal
Biography

Mohsen Abdel Hafeez Abdel Aal, an Egyptian journalist and artist is interested in writing and illustrating children's books. He is the author of more than 1000 books published in Egypt, the UAE, Saudi Arabia, Morocco, The United States and The United Kingdom, in Arabic and English languages. He is interested in communicating between different cultures, respect for humanity and love for the diverse animals with which we share the same environment.

This is the 4th book he has illustrated for author Mary Griffith Chalupsky.

Books By
Mary Griffith Chalupsky

JOGGER'S ADVENTURES

How Jogger Got His Name

Jogger Goes to School

Jogger Learns to Fish

Jogger Goes to the Circus

Christmas With Jogger

Jogger's Valentines

Jogger Drives Big Red

Jogger Goes to the Prom

Jogger Saves the Day

Jogger's New Friends

Jogger Goes to a Car Show

Jogger Goes to a Rodeo

Jogger's Birthday

A Bicycle for Jogger

Fun at the Amusement Park

The Littlest Puppy

Jimmy's Adventures

The Big, Bad, Sad, Mad Meany

Wings, Fins, a Bully and Friends, Book 1, 2

Puppy Pirates

Finding Christmas Spirit

Mary's Garden (a book of original poetry)

Tales from the Enchanted Forest, book 1, 2,3

Beyond the Rainbow Bridge

Mali, the Therapy Dog